AF469829

First published in 2007 by

KEVIN MAYHEW LTD
Buxhall, Stowmarket, Suffolk, IP14 3BW
E-mail: info@kevinmayhewltd.com
Website: www.kevinmayhew.com

9 8 7 6 5 4 3 2 1 0

ISBN 978 1 84417 760 8
Catalogue No. 1501005

Artwork by George & Angie Allen
Design by Chris Coe

Printed and bound in China

Contents ... the Old Testament

Contents ... the New Testament

Contents . . . the New Testament continued

Introduction
We hope you love
the stories in the
second My Bible
as much as we do.

For
Samuel, Luke and Sarah

The
Old Testament

Genesis	Ecclesiastes
Exodus	Song of Songs
Leviticus	Isaiah
Numbers	Jeremiah
Deuteronomy	Lamentations
Joshua	Ezekiel
Judges	Daniel
Ruth	Hosea
1 Samuel	Joel
2 Samuel	Amos
1 Kings	Obadiah
2 Kings	Jonah
1 Chronicles	Micah
2 Chronicles	Nahum
Ezra	Habakkuk
Nehemiah	Zephaniah
Esther	Haggai
Job	Zechariah
Psalms	Malachi
Proverbs	

Cain and Abel

Cain and Abel were brothers.

They were the children
of Adam and Eve.

Both made their living from the land,
Cain by growing crops and Abel by
keeping sheep and goats.

Each brought to God their produce,
but when God seemed to like Abel's
gift more, Cain became very angry.

God told him he must stop being so
jealous of Abel, but he could not.

He lured his brother into a field
and he killed him.

Genesis 4:1–12

Lot's wife

God had decided to destroy the
cities of Sodom and Gomorrah
because they were full of bad people,
but he did not want Lot
and his family to die.

He told them to leave their home
in Sodom and to neither stop
nor look back as they left it.

Lot's wife did not obey God,
and looking back, she was turned
into a pillar of salt.

Genesis 19:15–26

Hagar

Abraham had two sons,
Ishmael and Isaac.

Hagar, his wife's maid,
was Ishmael's mother and Sarah,
his wife, was Isaac's mother.

Before she was pregnant, Sarah had
told Abraham to have a child with
Hagar so that he would have an heir.

But when Sarah had a child of her own,
she forced Hagar and Ishmael to go
away, so that Isaac's inheritance would
not be shared with his half-brother.

God came to Hagar who was very
unhappy, and promised that Ishmael,
like Isaac, would prosper.

Genesis 21:1–21

Leah

Laban had two daughters,
Leah and Rachel.

Rachel was very beautiful and Jacob
wanted to marry her.

He asked Laban's permission, and
Laban agreed that if Jacob worked for
him for seven years they could marry.

When seven years had passed,
a marriage was arranged,
but Laban tricked Jacob,
putting Leah in Rachel's place.

Jacob then had to work another seven
years to be able to marry Rachel.

Genesis 29:16–30

Laban

Jacob looked after the sheep and goats belonging to his father-in-law, Laban.

When Jacob decided to return to his own country, he asked Laban for his payment.

They agreed that Jacob should have all the speckled animals so that he could start his own flock.

But Laban, a dishonest man, hid all the speckled sheep and goats far from the farm.

Jacob then had to stay and look after Laban's flock, waiting for the number of speckled animals to increase.

Genesis 30:25–43

The Passover

The Israelites were slaves in Egypt and wanted to leave, but Pharaoh, the Egyptian ruler, would not let them go.

Moses asked Pharaoh to free the Israelites, or God would kill the oldest child in every Egyptian family. But Pharaoh still refused to let them go.

God then sent an angel of death to every Egyptian house, but not to the Israelites.

Moses had told every Israelite family to put blood over the doors of their house so that the angel of death would pass over them.

That is why no Israelite children died and why the Jews celebrate a feast called the Passover.

Exodus 12:1–29

Balaam's donkey

God told Balaam not to go to Moab, where Balak ruled. At first Balaam was obedient, but it did not last.

As he was riding to Moab, his donkey stopped and would go no further.

No matter how much Balaam beat his donkey, it would not go forward.

Only when the donkey spoke to him did he realise it was God who was preventing his journey.

The donkey could see God's angel guarding the road ahead, but it was hidden to Balaam. Balaam was very sorry for disobeying God.

Numbers 22

Deborah

Deborah was a wise woman.

She was God's prophet,
but she was also a judge in Israel.

When she was working she would sit
under a particular palm tree so that
people would know where to find her.

There, she would give advice, even
advise the generals in times of war.

She is remembered because she,
under the guidance of God,
told the leader of Israel's army
how to defeat the Canaanites.

It was a great victory, and secured
peace in Israel for forty years.

Judges 4:1-16

Ruth and Naomi

Naomi lived with her daughters-in-law
Orpah and Ruth in Moab.

Their husbands had all died.

Orpah and Ruth had been born in
Moab, but Naomi was from Judah.

There was a famine in Moab and Naomi
decided to return to her home country.

She did not want Orpah and Ruth to
feel tied to her, and told them to stay
in Moab and find new husbands.

Orpah did so, but Ruth loved Naomi
so much that she would not be
separated from her.

Ruth 1:6–18

Hannah

Hannah was very sad.

She longed for a child,
but years passed and no child came.

Deeply unhappy, she promised God
that if she had a son she would bring
him up to serve him in the Temple.

God answered her prayer,
and she gave birth to a baby boy.

The boy was called Samuel.

When he was old enough,
Hannah kept her promise, and Samuel
went to live and work at the Temple.

1 Samuel 1:9–20

Jonathan

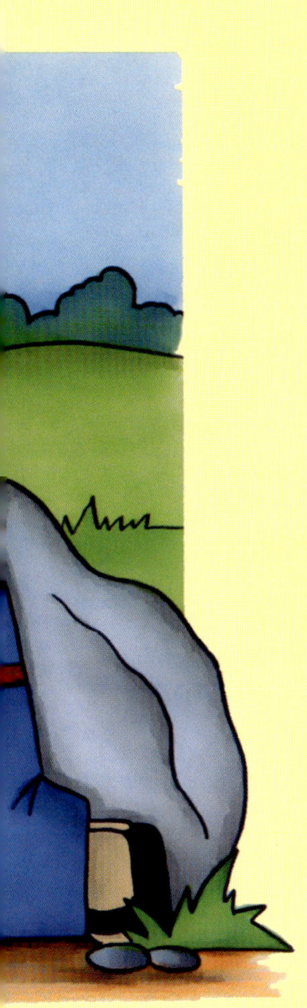

David and Jonathan were close friends,
but Jonathan's father,
King Saul, hated David.

He was jealous of David's popularity
after the killing of Goliath,
and wanted to kill him.

The friends therefore had a secret sign
to show when it was unsafe to meet.

If, when Jonathan was practising
archery, his arrow went beyond
a certain rock, David knew it was
unsafe to meet his friend.

1 Samuel 20:18–42

Abigail

Abigail's husband Nabal
insulted King David.

David was very angry and ordered his
soldiers to destroy Abigail's village.

Abigail thought quickly.

She went out to meet David and his
men with donkeys laden with gifts.

When she met them,
she offered what she had brought.

In this way, Abigail turned away their
anger and saved her village.

1 Samuel 25:18–25

The Queen of Sheba

The Queen of Sheba came to visit
King Solomon in Jerusalem.

She came in royal procession
with many signs of her great wealth
and importance.

She had heard of Solomon's
God-given wisdom and came to
test him with hard questions.

When she saw him, she asked
everything that was on her mind,
and he answered everything.

The Queen then knew that
Solomon's wisdom was from God.

1 Kings 10:11–13

Elijah

God told the prophet Elijah to tell Ahab, Israel's King, that there was going to be a drought because Israel had worshipped false gods.

Ahab did not believe him.

God then told Elijah to go and camp by the river Cherith.

Elijah did as God asked; he drank water from the river and ravens fed him with bread and meat.

Because no rain fell, the river eventually dried up, showing to Ahab the truth of Elijah's words.

1 Kings 17:1–7

The widow's oil

A woman whose husband had died found that she could not pay her bills.

The people she owed money to threatened to take her children away and sell them as slaves.

She asked Elisha for help.

All she had was a little bit of oil.

Elisha told her to borrow lots of empty jars and to start filling them from the jar containing her own oil.

Miraculously, her jar did not run out. She filled so many empty jars with oil that she had enough to sell and pay off all her debts.

2 Kings 4:1–7

The floating axe-head

Elisha went with a group of God's people to build new homes by the river.

While they were chopping down trees, one man's axe-head came off and dropped into the water.

He was very worried because the axe did not belong to him.

He asked Elisha to help.

Elisha cut a stick from a tree, threw it into the water where the axe-head had fallen, and the axe-head floated to the surface where the man could reach it.

2 Kings 6:5–7

Josiah

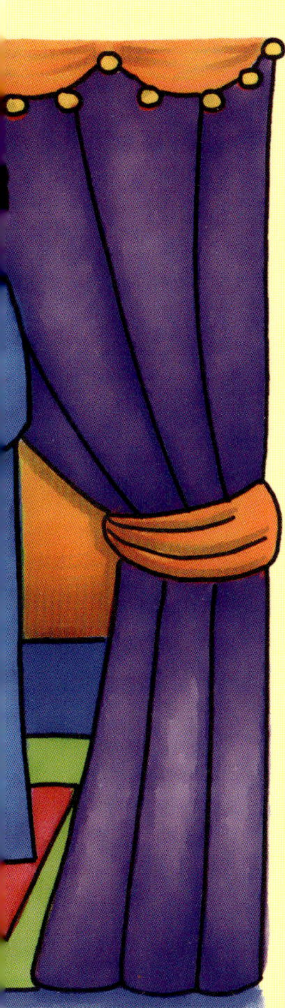

Josiah was only eight when his father
died and he became King of Israel.

Though young, he tried to do
God's will and was a good King.

He reigned for thirty-one years.

The most important event of his reign
was the finding of a book of God's laws.

It was found when the Temple
was being repaired.

Josiah tried to ensure it was read
and obeyed by everyone.

2 Kings 22:1–2

Nehemiah

Nehemiah was very sad that the Temple in Jerusalem was in ruins.

He was the governor of the city, which was ruled by Persia.

He asked the Persian King for permission to rebuild it.

The King said yes and Nehemiah travelled to the city to begin work.

He called upon the Jewish people to help him, and they did so in large numbers.

Nehemiah 2:1–5

Job

Job was a man who lost everything he had: his family, his home, his work, his property and even his health.

He only had rags to wear and was covered in sores.

His friends hardly recognised him, but they came and sat with him, and they tried to comfort him.

What they found could not be taken from Job was his faith in God.

Job 2:11–13

The good wife

The Bible teaches that a good wife
is to be deeply loved.

She is more precious than jewels,
she is trustworthy and works
constantly for the good of the family.

She is wise and humble before God.

She is a source of pride
for her husband
and for all who know her.

Proverbs 31:10–31

Jeremiah

Jeremiah was sent by God
to a potter's shop
to watch a potter at work.

He saw how, in the potter's hands,
the clay was sometimes made into a
beautiful pot and sometimes spoiled
and so reworked into something new.

God told Jeremiah that Israel was like
the clay in the potter's hand;
if the nation did not obey him,
he would destroy it in order
to shape something entirely new.

Jeremiah 18:1–10

Dry bones

God took Ezekiel the prophet
to a valley full of dry bones to show
Ezekiel that he had not forgotten
the people of Israel and that he
should not give up hope.

God asked him,
'Can these bones live?'

Ezekiel answered,
'Only you know, my God.'

God told him to call the bones to life.

Ezekiel did as God had asked,
and the dry bones were changed
into a crowd of people.

Ezekiel 37:1–10

Matthew
Mark
Luke
John
The Acts
Romans
1 Corinthians
2 Corinthians
Galatians
Ephesians
Philippians
Colossians
1 Thessalonians
2 Thessalonians

1 Timothy
2 Timothy
Titus
Philemon
Hebrews
James
1 Peter
2 Peter
1 John
2 John
3 John
Jude
Revelation

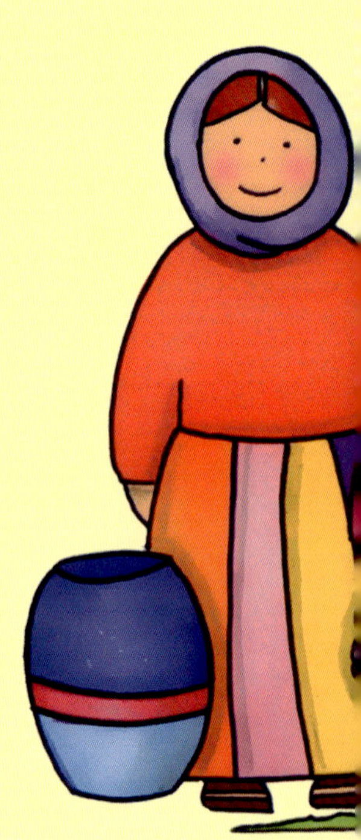

The
New Testament

Elizabeth meets Mary

Elizabeth and Mary were cousins.

Both were expecting a baby,
so that when they met, both were
excited and had much to say.

Their unborn children were gifts
of God; Elizabeth was old and thought
herself beyond childbearing,
and Mary was a virgin.

When the two met, the baby in
Elizabeth's tummy jumped for joy.

This was actually the first meeting
between John the Baptist and Jesus.

Luke 1:39-41

Joseph and Mary lose Jesus

When Jesus was 12, his parents took him to Jerusalem.

Travelling home with a large group of people, Mary and Joseph became very worried when they realised that Jesus was not with them.

They found him, eventually, in the Temple at Jerusalem, talking to the teachers about God.

They were cross and relieved at the same time, but Jesus did not apologise. Instead he said, 'Didn't you know I would be in my Father's house?' They didn't understand what he meant, but Mary did not forget his words.

Luke 2:41–50

Wilderness

Before Jesus started to teach people
about God, he took some time out
to think and pray.

He went into the desert and
stayed there for forty days
and forty nights without any food.

While he was there he was tempted
on three occasions to accept
a different way of life, one which would
mean disobeying God, but he resisted.

When he came out of the desert
he was a much stronger person.

Luke 4:1–2

Morning prayer

Times of prayer alone
with his heavenly Father
were central to Jesus' life.

He would get up
very early in the morning,
while it was still dark and
go somewhere to be on his own.

Untroubled by the presence
of other people, he was able
to draw close to God.

Mark 1:35–37

Hidden lights

Jesus teaches us that
Christians are like lights
in a dark world.

By looking at a Christian's life,
people begin to see
what God is like.

The Christian life
should not be hidden.

A light that is covered up
leaves everyone in the dark.

Matthew 5:14-15

The narrow way

Jesus taught his friends that
there are two paths to choose in life,
a wide one and a narrow one.

The wide path is easy,
and many people choose it.

If you think only of yourself,
do bad rather than good,
then that is the path you are on.

Walking the narrow path is much
harder and can be very lonely, but it is
the only path that leads to God.

It means choosing to love,
no matter what the cost.

Matthew 7:13-14

Wheat and weeds

To explain why both good and bad
people seem to prosper in the world,
Jesus told his friends a story about
a farmer who had wheat and weeds
growing in the same field.

His workers wanted to remove the
weeds immediately, but the farmer
told them to wait until harvest –
removing the weeds beforehand
could damage the good crop.

When God's harvest comes,
he will separate
what is good and bad.

Matthew 13:36–43

The coin in a fish's mouth

Sometimes Jesus would solve
problems in surprising ways.

Once, when money
was needed to pay a tax,
he told Peter to go to the lake
and throw out his line,
and then open the mouth
of the first fish he caught.

Inside, Peter found a coin;
enough to pay the tax
for Jesus and himself!

Matthew 17:24–27

A wicked servant

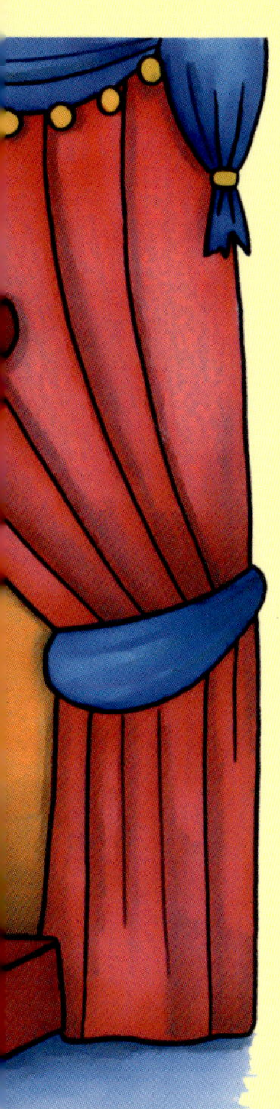

Jesus told this story to teach us about forgiveness; as we have been forgiven by God, so we should forgive one another.

A King told a servant who owed him a lot of money that he did not need to repay it.

The same servant was himself owed a small amount of money by a fellow servant.

Instead of following the King's example, he insisted on repayment.

The King was so angry he changed his mind about letting the servant off the money he owed.

Matthew 18:21–35

The fig tree

Jesus was hungry
and seeing a fig tree by the roadside
he went to pick some fruit from it.

Although the tree was in leaf,
it had no figs. Jesus said to it,
'May you never bear fruit again,'
and the tree died.

The disciples were amazed,
but Jesus told them
that if you have faith,
and do not doubt, you will receive
whatever you ask for in prayer.

Matthew 21:18–22

Lamps

In the time of Jesus, weddings could last all day and the bridegroom could come at any time.

The bridegroom would be greeted by young women holding flaming oil-filled lamps.

Jesus told his friends he would return like a bridegroom coming to a wedding, and that they must be like lampbearers waiting for him.

They should be prepared to wait like the wise lampbearers who had taken extra oil with them.

It would be foolish to run out of oil and miss the opportunity to greet the bridegroom.

Matthew 25:1-13

75

Talents

Jesus told this story to show that the gifts God gives should be used, not hidden away.

A rich man gave his servants money to invest while he was away.

On his return the rich man called for his servants.

He praised and gave rewards to all except one servant who, instead of investing the money, had hidden it in the ground.

The rich man was very angry with this servant.

He took the money back from him and gave him the sack.

Matthew 25:14-30

77

Corn on the Sabbath

One Sabbath,
when Jesus and his friends were
walking through cornfields, they were
seen picking corn and eating it.

According to strict Jewish Law
this was wrong, because Jews
were not allowed to do any work
on the Sabbath, even something
as small as hand-picking corn.

Jewish Law-Keepers began to criticise
Jesus, but he reminded them that the
spirit of the Law is more important
than the letter by saying,
'The Sabbath was made for man,
not man for the Sabbath.'

Mark 2:23–28

A seed of mustard

The mustard seed is the smallest
of all seeds – just like a grain of sand
in the hand – but once planted,
from it grows a really big tree.

When you look at the tiny seed,
it is hard to imagine that a tree large
enough for birds to settle
in its branches can come from it.

Jesus tells us that faith is like that;
the tiniest grain of faith
can achieve incredible things.

Mark 4:30–32

Legion

One evening Jesus crossed by boat
to a beach on the eastern side
of the Sea of Galilee.

He was met by a
very frightening man called Legion.

Legion was so disturbed in his mind
that he could not be with other people
and lived instead in the graveyard
among the tombs.

In the same way that Jesus had
commanded a storm on the lake to be
still, so he commanded the storm in the
man's mind to be still and at peace.

The man's peace of mind
was completely restored.

Mark 5:1-20

The centurion's faith

A Roman centurion asked Jesus
to come to his home to pray
for his servant who was dying.

Before Jesus arrived, however,
the centurion had sent a message
to him saying, 'I am not worthy to
receive you, but pray for my servant
and he will be healed.'

The centurion believed that the
prayers of Jesus were like the orders
he gave to his soldiers, he only needed
to ask and it would happen.

And so it was; Jesus prayed
and the servant recovered.

Luke 7:1–10

A woman's gratitude

In Jesus' time it was a sign of respect for a visitor's feet to be washed.

When Jesus entered Simon's house, Simon neglected to fulfil the custom, but a woman who had lived a bad life did it in his place.

She washed Jesus' feet with her tears, dried them with her hair, and anointed them with expensive perfume.

Her actions went far beyond what was expected because they were not the actions of duty but of love.

Jesus told the woman, 'Because you have done this, your sins are forgiven.'

Luke 7:36–50

Jesus' cloak

Jesus was surrounded by people
who wanted to be near him.

On one occasion he was being jostled
by the crowd when suddenly
he became aware that his coat had
been deliberately pulled from behind.

He discovered that a woman
who was ill and who had been bleeding
for twelve years was responsible.

She had grasped his coat
because she believed that by
doing so she would be healed.

Her faith was rewarded,
and Jesus told her to go in peace.

Luke 8:43-48

89

Neighbours

A Bible teacher
came to Jesus and asked him,
'What must I do to go to heaven?'
Jesus said,
'What does the Bible say?'
The man answered,
'Love God and love
your neighbour as yourself.'

Jesus told him that he
had given the right answer,
but went on to say that knowing
the right answer is not enough
– you have to do it.

Luke 10:25–28

A wonderful meal

Jesus told a story.

An important man once prepared a great meal to which he invited many rich and powerful people, but no one turned up.

He sent his servants to find out why, and all his guests gave excuses.

So, not wanting to eat alone, he asked his servants to invite the poor, the sick and the homeless to dine with him.

They came and had a wonderful meal.

The story reminds us not to miss out when Jesus invites us to a party.

Luke 14:16–24

The lost coin

When we lose something valuable,
we search high and low
until we find it.

We can therefore understand
how a woman felt when
she lost a valuable silver coin,
and how happy she was
to find it again.

Her happiness, Jesus said,
is like the happiness in heaven
when a person begins to love God.

Luke 15:8–10

An infectious disease

One day when Jesus was
going to Jerusalem he met ten men
with an infectious skin disease.

People were afraid and stayed
away from them.

The men asked Jesus to heal them.

He told them to go and see the priest.

As they went, they were all made well.

Although all of them
should have been grateful to God,
only one came back to say thank you.

Luke 17:11–19

The rich young ruler

A rich young ruler asked Jesus
what trusting God meant.

Jesus told him that he must first
follow all God's laws.

The young man told him
that he already did this.

'Then,' said Jesus, 'you must sell all
you have and give it to the poor.'

This made the man sad
because he was very rich.

Jesus was asking him to depend
completely on God, and for the rich
young man that was asking too much.

Luke 18:18–25

A widow's pennies

One day Jesus was in the Temple
watching people putting money
into a collecting box.

A poor widow put in just two pennies
because it was all she could afford.

Jesus drew attention to her,
not because of how little she had given,
but because of how much.

Her gift left her with nothing.

Generosity, he told his friends,
is not only about how much you give,
but how much you keep.

Luke 21:1-4

God alone can judge

Jesus was teaching in the Temple.

While he was there the religious teachers brought in a woman who had done something so wrong that she was to be stoned to death.

Jesus believed only God could judge people. He asked for a person who had done no wrong to throw the first stone.

Of course, everybody left at that point and the woman went free.

It is a reminder that none of us is perfect, and that God alone judges truly.

John 8:3–11

True service

One evening Jesus did something
very special for his closest friends.

He took off his robe,
knelt down in front of them,
took some water and a towel,
and he washed and dried their feet.

This was a job usually done
by the servant of the house.

By doing this he wanted them
to understand that
to serve people is to love them.

John 13:4-7

The vine

Sometimes when Jesus taught
he used words to draw pictures.

'I am like a grapevine,' he once told
his friends, 'and God is like
the gardener looking after me.'

He then told them that they were
like the branches of the vine
bearing the grapes,
but that they could only produce fruit
if they stayed attached to him.

John 15:1-8

Jesus on the beach

When Jesus died, his friends
did not expect to see him again,
but on Easter Day
God brought Jesus back to life.

After that, whenever
his friends met him, they were
always surprised and very happy.

They discovered that whatever
they were doing, he was with them,
whether they were at work fishing
or on the beach eating breakfast.

John 21:9

Stephen

Stephen was not afraid
to speak about Jesus, even though
it made him very unpopular.

According to Jewish law,
by saying that Jesus is God's Son,
he was guilty of blasphemy.

The punishment for this
was death by stoning.

Stephen was stoned to death,
but just like Jesus,
as he died he asked for those
who threw the stones to be forgiven.

Acts 7:54-60

The Damascus road

Saul was a Jew who hated Christians.

He got permission from the priests in Jerusalem to go to Damascus to arrest and bring back to Jerusalem any Christians he found there.

Just before he arrived, however, a bright light blinded him, and he was not able to see for three days.

God spoke to him through his blindness, and he realised that he had been blind to the truth about Jesus.

As soon as he understood this, his sight returned and he was baptised as a Christian.

Acts 9:1-19

Setting prisoners free

King Herod had Peter locked up
in a secure prison, and intended
to have him put to death.

However, the whole church
prayed for Peter,
and something wonderful happened.

During the night an angel came
to the prison, woke Peter up,
released him from his chains,
and led him out to safety.

Peter thought it was a dream,
and so did his family and friends
when he knocked at the door.

But it was not a dream; God,
through his angel, had set him free.

Acts 12:1–10

115

Lydia

Lydia was a woman
who ran a market stall.

She believed in God,
and every Saturday she went to
a quiet place by the river to pray.

On one such visit,
Paul was there talking about Jesus.

She listened and became convinced
that what he was saying was true.

She put her trust in Jesus and she
and all her family were baptised.

Acts 16:13–15

Shipwrecked!

Having been arrested, Paul was put on a ship for trial in Rome.

The sea journey was long, and part-way through it, the winds were so severe that steering the ship became impossible.

The passengers and crew were frightened of drowning.

Only Paul remained calm, because God had told him in a dream that though the ship would be lost, all who sailed with him would be kept safe.

That is what happened.

The ship was wrecked off the coast of Malta but God saved the life of everyone on board.

Acts 27:13-44

God's armour

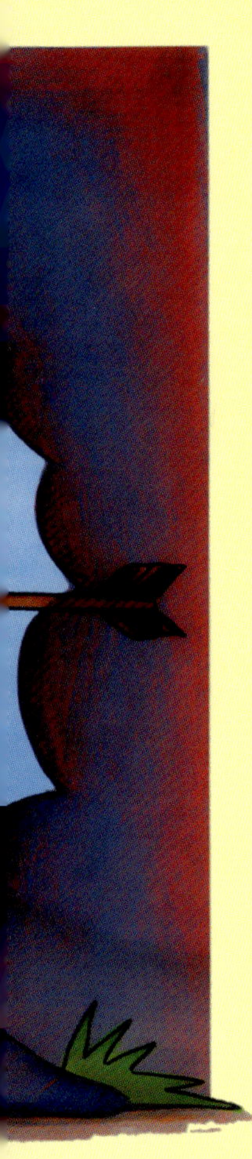

Paul told his friends that the world
can be a dangerous place,
but God has given his people
gifts to keep them safe.

God's own friendship,
the good news about Jesus,
faith, truth and the Bible are,
he tells them,
like a soldier's suit of armour,
their protection in the battles of life.

Ephesians 6:10–18

Jesus, bright like the sun

One day Jesus will return to the world.

When John was on the island
of Patmos, he had a dream
in which he was carried to the future
and saw what Jesus would look like
when he returned.

Jesus was radiant like the sun;
his hair was pure white,
his eyes were like fire,
his chest shone with gold and his voice
was like the sound of rushing water.

Revelation 1:12–16

Jesus at the door!

Jesus is very polite.

Just like us, before going
into the room of someone important,
he knocks and waits.

We are important to Jesus,
and our hearts are like a room
into which he would like to come.

Jesus is knocking and
waiting for an answer.

Will we let him in?

Revelation 3:20

The New Jerusalem

The old city of Jerusalem was
destroyed by the Romans in AD 70.

John may actually have seen it happen.

In a vision of heaven,
John saw the city rebuilt, made new,
with gold and precious stones
built into its walls.

In contrast to the old city,
it was a place of healing and peace,
where there was no pain,
or death or tears.

Revelation 21

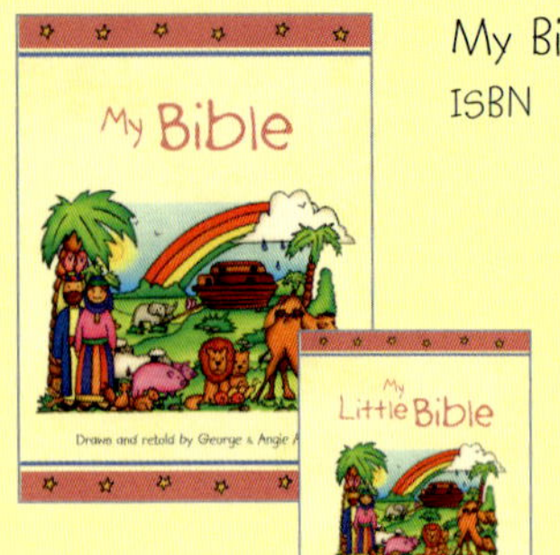

My Bible
ISBN 978 1 84417 683 0

My Little Bible
Hardback: ISBN 978 1 84417 728 8
Paperback: ISBN 978 1 84417 727 1

Other wonderful books
by George and Angie Allen

My Bible Colouring Book 1
ISBN 978 1 84417 691 5

My Bible Colouring Book 2
ISBN 978 1 84417 692 2

My Bible Colouring Book 3
ISBN 978 1 84417 693 9

My Bible Colouring Book 4
ISBN 978 1 84417 694 6

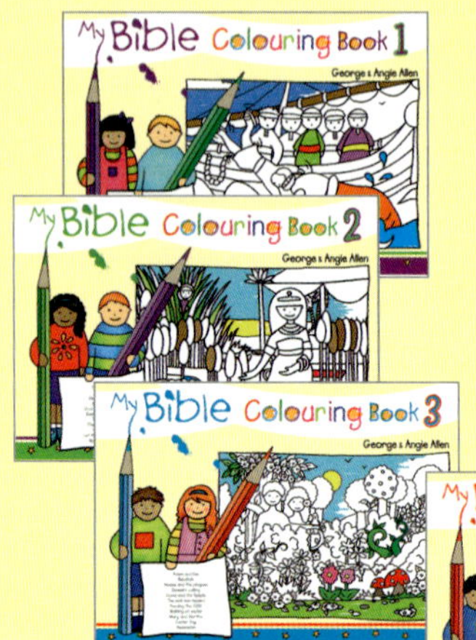

My Bible 2 Colouring Book 1
ISBN 978 1 84417 761 5

My Bible 2 Colouring Book 2
ISBN 978 1 84417 762 2

My Bible 2 Colouring Book 3
ISBN 978 1 84417 763 9

My Bible 2 Colouring Book 4
ISBN 978 1 84417 764 6